To the Sacketts:

Please don't be

"that"

person!! :)

Enjoy these stories!! :)

Kevin J Heppell

Nightmare
In The Drive Thru

True and Untold Stories from the Fast Food Industry

Kevin J. Hopler

ISBN: 978-1-4834-4417-8 (sc)
ISBN: 978-1-4834-4416-1 (e)

Because of the dynamic nature of the Internet, any web addresses or links contained in this book may have changed since publication and may no longer be valid. The views expressed in this work are solely those of the author and do not necessarily reflect the views of the publisher, and the publisher hereby disclaims any responsibility for them.

Any people depicted in stock imagery provided by Thinkstock are models, and such images are being used for illustrative purposes only. Certain stock imagery © Thinkstock.

Lulu Publishing Services rev. date: 07/11/2016

CONTENTS

FOREWORD

I often tell teenagers looking for a summer job to apply for a job in the fast food industry. I tell them that they will make a few extra bucks, make a few extra friends, and get a whole pile of new stories that they will tell for the rest of their lives. As I look back at the four years when I was a teenager working in this industry, I have nothing but great memories and great stories. Kevin manages to share these memories and tell these stories in a way which everyone feels like they are "inside" of the inside joke. I truly hope these stories give you as much enjoyment and laughter as they did for me as I lived them many, many summers ago.

Ryan Unick

"Human Meat"

This older lady walked in one evening, placed her order and sat down and began eating it. After a few minutes of eating, she walked back up to the teenager that took his order and yelled at him, "I said I wanted beef in my burger!"

The teenager looked at her and said, "Excuse me? What do you mean?"

She told him that she didn't want to eat burgers made out of "human meat!"

He assured her that it was all beef and it was not made of human. She said to him, "Don't lie to me! I see the machines in the back!"

He replied, "Ma'am, that machine dispenses fries!"

She continued to yell at him that we hired people to serve them as sandwiches, he started becoming emotional. The manager had to walk over and handle the situation, reassuring her that the meat used was beef, not human.

She was thinking that we hired people just to kill them and serve them as burgers. It's no wonder why we had a "Now Hiring" sign on the window.

PROLOGUE

Many people remember the infamous lawsuit in the early 1990's of the woman suing a popular restaurant because of her coffee being "too hot." If you don't remember the story, well here it is. An elderly woman went through the drive thru ordering a coffee with the cream and the sugar on the side. She preceded to put the coffee between her knees to put the cream and sugar inside, took off the lid and low and behold, it spilled all over her, thus becoming someone else's fault. It brought a lot of "heat," (pun definitely intended) on this restaurant and all other companies in the industry, bringing to light the burning question, "How hot is too hot?"

Consider this: for years many people have been consuming the same coffee, at the same temperature, in the same cup. The only difference was the circumstances for this specific series of events. She spilled the coffee on her lap after taking the lid off and having it between her knees. Most people would wait until they are in a stable environment to do this, whether the coffee is hot, room temperature or cold.

The more disturbing fact is the lawsuit only took into consideration that she was only 20% liable. If there is steam coming off, it means it is HOT! If you need to cool it down, ask for a cup of ice, blow on it, or wait for it to cool down.

Some customers have broken down windows to get chicken nuggets, thrown temper tantrums because they arrived after breakfast ended, and even brought a gun with them because they claimed to have been missing a cheeseburger. This book will look at the customers that make even the happiest employees cringe to serve, along with some cheerful stories. These stories are of the scariest, worst, and dumbest customers that make everyday life harder. Hopefully, this book will give you a better understanding that the way you act towards others makes a difference, no matter the job. I also hope it makes you laugh, or at the least give you something to think about. Let's start off with a bang:

CHAPTER 1

Did That Really Happen?

"He's got an ax! Or a machete! Or a knife! Or... Something!"

One morning, I was training a new manager how to open. Everything was going smoothly, for the first 45 minutes, until this guy came through the drive through. I asked what I could get him, and he told me that his wallet was wet, and he had no money so he wanted me to give him everything for free. I said to him that I was sorry, but I couldn't do that. He proceeded to yell at me and tell me that he's here every day and that he was going to get his food, one way or another. I had never seen him before. The woman who was behind him waited a few minutes then decided to just drive around him to the window. She gave me her order of oatmeal and so I took her money thinking the guy at the speaker was just an old man going senile, and I was right. He drove around and parked in front of the young lady blocking her off from escape. He decided to scream at me thinking that fear of being screamed at would be his best arrow in his quiver of free food. Well, apparently he had something else next to the quiver because as I'm in the middle of making her oatmeal, I hear the phrase, "Oh my God, he's got a knife! Call the cops!"

It was at that point where I walk over to the window and long and behold, he was swinging something in his hand. At this point, I called the police so they could just deal with this ax bearer. As the police were on their way, the guy entered the building, scaring all the employees making them run to the back, in fear of their lives. He came inside screaming about how he wanted hash browns. After realizing there was no one to

1

help him, because he's crazy, he walked back outside and saw the police cars arrive. He walked out and started talking to them, not knowing they were called there because of him. They talked to him then removed him from the premises. I have to admit though, the lady was tough. She sat through this whole ordeal then was questioned about the incident by the police and afterwards asked us, "Can I just have my oatmeal?"

I responded, "Oh yes. I forgot about that." She went through too much for oatmeal. I think she overpaid.

We were all talking about this incident after it happened. I just looked at the manager in training and said to her, "Normal Tuesday! This stuff happens all the time." I hope she realized I was just kidding.

"Don't Bank on the Bank"

Early in the morning, a guy walked in and placed a decent sized order. He paid with a twenty dollar bill and got change back. He started telling the person that took his order that he paid with a fifty dollar bill, not a twenty. The employee was sure it was only a twenty so the manager was brought in the mix. The guy insisted that he just came from the bank and the bank wouldn't make a mistake like that. When change is in question, we count the drawer to double check. If the drawer was over by their change amount, they would get their change. The manager counted the drawer, and it came out even. The manager told the customer it was even; the customer became irate. He started cursing and swearing at them, told them that they're thieves, and said that the employee stole and to check their pockets. The customer eventually got so angry that he took the bag of food that he bought and threw it at the manager, missing the manager by a lot but hitting a sign dead-on, breaking the sign. The cops were called out and eventually the guy was forced to pay for the new sign. His morning ended with a phone call from the bank telling him that they accidently gave him a twenty instead of a fifty and apologized for the mistake.

Moral of this story: Whoops!

"Pants on Fire"

I had someone come in really early in the morning, and she ordered a few items. She paid with a twenty and so I gave her change for the twenty. After I gave her the change, she told me that she gave me a fifty. She wanted the change for a fifty dollar bill. I was positive that I gave her the right change. I told her that she only handed me a twenty but she was insistent that she handed me a fifty. So I called the manager over and told him just to open the drawer. He opened it and I said to her, "There are no fifties in the drawer and just you're one twenty."

She immediately quieted down and said nothing as she was caught in a lie.

"For Your 18th Birthday, I Will Give You a Jail Threat!"

A few days after my 18th birthday, I worked the window taking money and handing out food. This older couple came through in a minivan and placed an order. They drove up to the window, paid with a ten dollar bill and so I gave them their change, food, and drinks. They told me that I short-changed them by ten dollars, and they paid with a twenty dollar bill. I told them they paid with a ten. After a minute of talking to the customer, I brought over the manager, and he told them to park out of the line while he counted the drawer. After he counted the drawer, the drawer was even. The manager then walked out to the parked car, told them that the drawer was even, and there was nothing he could do for them. The people then insisted that I stole the money and to check my pockets, like everyone says when they're angry, and told the manager, "If you don't give me my money I will call the police and have that kid arrested. Do you know who I am? I am blah, blah, blah, blah, blah!"

To diffuse the situation, the manager just pulled out ten dollars of his OWN money and handed it to him.

It's amazing how many people think that the police force is there to enforce their set of rules other than doing what's right.

"Bubblegum Machine, Can You Take My Order?"

We had a bubblegum machine for kids. You put in a quarter and out popped bubblegum balls. It also said things like, "Welcome!" and "Have a good one!" Well, late one night, there were only a handful of employees in the store, and the person that was supposed to be up front, walked to the back to clean a piece of equipment. Less than a minute later, he returned to an irate customer that had to wait a few seconds for his order to be taken. When speaking to the manager about the "incident," if you want to even call it that, the guy responded, "I had to wait forever to be taken care of and when my order was taken, the bubblegum machine spoke more English then my server did." **WOW**

Moral of **THIS** story: He wanted to order some bubblegum!

"Hot, Hot, Hot… Or Cold"

A morning there was a customer that came through the drive-thru and asked for a large hot iced tea. After a second, the order taker asked what they wanted to confirm what they said, and I chimed in, "They said they wanted a large hot iced coffee! Wait a second…" Feeling dumb, I continued, "How would we do that?"

It made me think back to the days of Saturday Night Live's "Celebrity Jeopardy" skit where "Ricky Martin" gave the clue when he was asked if the "hot tea" was "hot hot hot or cold."

"Screwdriver You"

On a hot, muggy summer afternoon, a young man with a jeep, without air-conditioning, came through the drive thru. He ordered food and we were waiting a minute for fries. So with no one behind him for the time being, I told him it was just a minute for fries and closed the window. A few seconds later, I heard a sound coming from the window. I saw him trying to open the window so I walked over and he had a screwdriver in his hand. I opened the window, and the screwdriver hit me in the finger. He said to me that we shouldn't be "hogging all the cool air from the air-conditioner" and that he's hot.

Way to be a jackass, sir.

"No Change for You!"

A lady came through while having two windows opened. The first window is where you pay, and the second window is where you pick up your order. Well, the woman gave the money at the first window and immediately left to the second window to pick up the order. About an hour after getting her food, she came back through the drive thru and screamed and yelled at the employee in the window. Her complaint was simple. She said that the person taking money never gave her the change owed to her and she was angry. We calmed her down by giving her the fifteen cents she thought she was owed.

I mean, we didn't need or want that money anyway.

"Put On Your Happy Face"

A bunch of teenagers walked in after school one time. Well, one day they decided to use their purchased food as art. They took their sandwiches to the booth, unwrapped it and, well, one thing led to another. The pickles became the eyes, the ketchup was the smile, and the rest of the burger became other parts of the smiley face on the w all.

I guess it could have been more inappropriate, but it was still a pain to clean off.

"Soccer Game Fiasco"

A woman came through the drive thru and ordered a lot of food, including, at least four kid's meals, four adult meals, two salads and many drinks. I took her money and handed her a salad and drinks and told her, "Hold on for the rest of your food."

I then turned around to ready the rest of her food and hand it to her. I turned back around with her food in hand and she's gone, just gone. She left with, at least, twenty dollars of her food in my hand. About 20 minutes later, we received a phone call from the lady that forgot her food. She called up yelling and screaming at the manager because we "forgot" to hand her the food she bought. We told her she could come and pick it up, and we will even make new food for her but she had to take her children to soccer practice and couldn't leave and her kids will now be hungry and we're all incompetent. She wanted us to deliver the food to her because we "messed up" but since we don't deliver, she felt we purposely made her forget her food.

She's right. "This is a customer, we wanted to go upset and tick off. Instead of spitting into food, we just won't give her the food she requested and paid for!" said sarcastically!

If you ever are running late and need to use the drive thru, please double check the order, use the receipt, and make sure you're done.

If you don't have time to redo a task, then get it right the first time.

CHAPTER 2
Yes, That Really Happened!

"Made Up Menu Items"

On the menu for desserts, it said sundae with fudge, strawberry, and caramel all on separate lines because they were different flavors. A woman came through and asked for a strawberry-fudge sundae. The order taker said, "I'm sorry. What did you want?"

She said again, "You know. A strawberry-fudge sundae. But no strawberries."

Really?

"Give Me What I Want, Not What I Say"

This happens a lot! A guy came through and asked for a cup of ice cream. We gave him a cup of ice cream. The guy asked, "Where's the chocolate syrup?"

Asking for a fudge sundae and a cup of ice cream are two separate things.

And then this other time…

A customer walked up to the register and asked for the steak bagel meal and wanted a coffee with it. Then, after he paid, he complained because he wanted just the sandwich, not the meal. He said meal and asked for a specific number then the employee clarified it and asked if he wanted the sandwich or the meal.

We always got it wrong, because after he paid, he changed what he wanted, and it was our fault.

6

"Lines Are For Losers"

Normally, when you get in line, you stay in line, especially when you're driving. Well, one afternoon, I took this guy's order and told him to drive around to the second window. There was a woman in front of him that was counting her money, getting ready to give it to us and didn't realize the line moved. The driver interpreted the phrase "drive to the second window," as pass everyone else waiting in line. So he drove around everyone in line and came up to the second window. Everyone else, at that point in time, was behind him, got upset and honked at him. He stood up for himself, and threw me under the bus simultaneously, and stuck his head out the window and yelled, "He told me to drive to the second window and I did!"

Thanks pal! With friends like you, who needs enemies?!

"Don't Forget Your... Where Did You Go?"

A customer walked in and placed an order for three grilled chicken meals and wanted it "to go." He paid for it. He picked up his drinks and told me that he wanted to take his drinks to the car and he would be right back. Well, he was never right back, or back at all. He left and somehow forgot his food.

It's amazing how you could forget something like that when you walk out.

"No Win Scenario" ("Kobayashi Maru")

This guy came in late at night and ordered 10 double cheeseburgers with only ketchup. We made his burgers and had everything ready, and then he pulled up. He told us he wanted everything fresh and not what we made him. Now, it took about three or four minutes just for the meat to be freshly made. It took, in total, about five minutes for everything to be made. Well, this didn't make matters better because now he was pissed for waiting so long. He didn't understand that when he came up to the window, refused his food, and wanted it fresh, he had to wait. He gave me a piece of his mind, it may have been his whole mind with the way he was talking, he took his food, asked my name, and said he was going to get me fired. The next day, I found out I was a dick by the store manager because the guy called the store, said his side of the story, and, without asking me my side, told me I mishandled the guy because I never gave my full name.

Even James T. Kirk couldn't reprogram his way out of this one.

"This Is Jeopardy"

This woman came through the drive thru and ordered a few hamburgers with nothing on it. I personally made it with another person so I knew there was nothing on it. After the order was finished, I went into the office to count money in some the drawers and do some paperwork when I started hearing yelling and screaming. This woman fed those burgers to her dog and said there were onions on it and that onions were poisonous and going to kill her dog. Now, I never heard of this before. Besides, I'm thinking, "I understand people thinking that they have to feed their dog "human food," but you should watch what you feed them. Fast food doesn't come in bags that say "Iams.""

Remember, I thought that and didn't say anything; I'm not that dumb. So, a day or two later, I was watching "Jeopardy," and they have a related clue. They answered, "This vegetable is poisonous to dogs," or something like that, and the question ended up being "What is onions?"

My "Jeopardy" thought to that was, "The person that didn't see that one coming," with the question, "Who is me?"

"Hit the Building and Run!"

So, these kids came through drive thru, ordered, paid and received their food. On their way out, they thought it would be funny to deafen the order taker and took out an air horn and blasted it in her ear then quickly left so not to be caught. They didn't realize we had a description of their car and of them. They also didn't think to turn their wheel away from the direction of the building. When they hit the gas, they hit the side of the building, then in a brilliant move, said. "Oh crap, let's get out of here!" and left.

A few minutes after this all happened, we called the police on the hit and run, and they were brought back to apologize. Even kids with their newly minted driver's licenses should realize that hit-and-runs are stupid, illegal, and can cost you!

"I'm Paying for Me and the Cop Behind Me"

The location of the store was/is next to a residential street, and since it's in New Jersey and the general consensus about speed limits is that they are only suggestions, people got pulled over a lot. One person pulled in through the drive thru line and didn't realize that there was a cop behind him with his lights flashing. We took the guy's order and the next car in line was the cop. When we asked for his order, he responded, "Nothing thanks, I'm just here to pull this guy in front of me over for speeding."

Alright, just drive around then!

"Can You Hear Me Now?"

An afternoon, I was taking orders in drive thru during a busy lunch. This older woman came in to order a small coffee. It was still brewing so they told her to take a seat, and they would bring it to her when it finished. About 10 minutes later, she came back up to the counter and started screaming and yelling in my direction. After a minute or so, she started cursing and finger pointing, they made her the coffee, and she sat down. The finger pointing was a dead giveaway that she was talking to me. Well, that and when asked to whom she was talking, she said that guy in the purple shirt. (Yes, I wore purple! It's a good looking color for a good looking man! Anyway…) When she sat down, I had a few people walk up to me and ask me what I did to deserve that. I told them I didn't know what they were talking about, and I didn't take any orders inside. They told me what happened and that the woman came up to yell at me for something I didn't do, and it got quite loud. I asked them who took her order and told her to sit down, and it was someone that looked and sounded nothing like me.

No one understood how I didn't hear her except the fact that I'm very oblivious to everything around me, and shortly later, they started wondering if I ever listen to anything they tell me. I'll give you a hint: everything goes in one ear, and out the other!

"Please Use the Toilet, Not the Sink"

An older person walked in almost every day to just get a senior coffee, sat down for a little while, got a refill once in a while, and then left. One day, in the afternoon, he came in to get his coffee and went outside to lie on the ground. After a while, he received the call of nature and came inside and immediately ran to the bathroom. Now, knowing people, you wouldn't think someone would do what's coming next, but it really did happen. He walked in the bathroom, walked up to the sink, pulled down his trousers, stuck his butt over the sink and **LET. HIMSELF. GO.** It went everywhere. We knew he did it, because on his way out, he was covered in it, and he stepped in some, and the trail followed to where he was laying in the grass.

That was just a "crappy" thing to do because someone has got to clean it up and you better believe it wasn't him.

"Destruction Solves Nothing!"

This isn't about customers, at least I hope not customers, but it does need saying. After a year or so of working there, one day I came in and saw that people, the night before, came after the store closed and broke and spray painted the windows and speaker box, and just generally, caused destruction. They wrote things about murder on the side of the building in spray paint.

Now, there is no justification out there, NONE, for this kind of behavior from "civilized" human beings. If you do not agree with a company or product, don't purchase it. Each dollar spent is supporting that company.

If you don't agree with an aspect of civilization, there are many nonviolent ways to protest, and needless destruction shouldn't be one of them.

"How Can I Make You Happy?"

We were busy enough, one night, the manager took money and handed food out. One customer came up, and the manager took his money, gave him his change and, well, you know where this is going. He claimed he didn't get the right amount of change back. The manager told him that he received the correct change but just to be sure, he counted the register. He did and it came up even. He told the guy that it was correct, but he didn't want to hear that, he wanted to hear, "Here's some money."

Well, the guy then became indignant on the manager and started yelling at him for this "incident." He then told him that even his double cheeseburger didn't have bacon on it. It didn't come with bacon because he didn't ask for bacon. The customer then left in a huff. He called the manager bad names before he left and threw him into a level of pissed off I had never seen. The manager ran outside chasing after him screaming, "Come back! Come back! How can I make you happy?!"

Greatest moment ever when you're not the person on the receiving end!

CHAPTER 3

The Parenting Guide on What Not To Do

"How Did You Do That?"

A while ago, these kids walked in and asked us if they could go on the roof. We said no because it was too dangerous, and we were liable for people that do that. So we left it at that, or so we thought. Apparently, a ball got stuck in the sign on the store over two stories up. My first thought was, "How did it get up there?"

They had to have been playing in the street with it or in the parking lot, but none of them looked like they could have gotten it that high. They were insistent that they needed to go on the roof to get their ball. Again, we said no because it was too dangerous. They decided to leave and found the ladder themselves and began to climb up. We quickly ran outside and told them to get down. After a little while, they left and we left and apparently they waited until we closed and nobody was around before they stupidly climbed up and got their ball.

Still, no one knows how the ball got stuck up there, and we will NEVER know.

"Parents Stupidity Creates Crash"

On a rainy day, a parent brought her kid in so that he could enjoy the PlayPlace. Now, before we go in to what happened, a few things must be known. One: We have a giant sign that tells the rules of the PlayPlace, and they range from the ages of kids that should be in there to common sense like, "Do not climb on the outside of the PlayPlace!" Two: Most parents don't read these signs and think that they are just suggestions that they don't have to abide by. Three: Most parents just don't pay attention to their kids when they are playing.

Now that we have that out of the way, we can get back to what happened.

The child was climbing on the outside of the PlayPlace and the parent, not knowing the rules or having any common sense, was not paying attention at all. Broke two rules simultaneously, wow. The child began to climb on the outside of the PlayPlace and climbed all the way up to the point that he was using the outside poles like monkey bars. The kid lost his grip and fell to the ground. After being rushed to the hospital, we found out that the kid had a broken arm.

Sounds like something that shouldn't be too much more involved with us, I mean the parent wasn't supervising the kid and let him climb to the top, swinging, and we're not any sort of "parent police" or anything. A few weeks later, I found out that the parent wanted us to pay part of their medical bills.

This implies partial blame on our part. Now, I don't mind using insurance to assist with their medical bills, but it was an incident that could have been avoided. I didn't know it was necessary to have employees out there making sure that parents are watching their children.

Surprisingly, there are parents that approve of this and actually help their kids climb on the outside because it is just so much darn fun riding in an ambulance.

"Be a Parent, Not a Friend"

This woman came up to counter after ordering. Her kids were misbehaving and she didn't want to stand up to her kids and tell them to stop. She came up to me and asked me to yell at them for her. I told her that I wasn't their parent and that she needed to do it herself. She tried to make me feel bad because I wouldn't help her kids behave. She asked again and in calm, nonthreatening voice, "Stop that."

She said to me, "Thank you." To her kids, "See! You just got yelled at by the manager!"

Sooner or later, parents like that have to realize, you don't want other people to raise your kids. Instead, grow up and realize that being a parent doesn't always mean being a friend.

"Boys Will Be... Well, Not Men"

These kids came in one afternoon and couldn't keep their mouths shut. They stood in line and there was a couple, woman and man, behind them. The woman was what is called in, men's terms, "gifted," which means a nice set of "bazookas." (Sometimes I'm ashamed to be a guy and know that.) One of the kids turned to the other and said quite loudly, to the point where everyone in the tri-state area heard him, "Dude, look at the rack on the woman behind us!"

Well, this is an incident that shouldn't have happened for two reasons. 1) Women deserve respect and shouldn't be noticed purely on their looks, but their mind as well. 2) The woman's boyfriend was right there, and you know most men don't take too kindly to that.

Of course, the guy walked up and told them to knock it off. The kids then thought it was not their fault so told him to mind his manners. The children sat down and started screaming curse words and began rough housing. It escalated to the point that, when an employee was going to go out to say something to them about their behavior, another customer decided to call the police on them and they were escorted out.

The kids were the ones "gifted" that day. (With a lesson in respect!)

"Babysitters"

One of our employees actually became a babysitter for a short period of time. A lady came in with her child and ordered some food. They took the food to the PlayPlace and ate their food. At eleven o'clock, we closed the store and there was no adult in the store. Everyone was getting ready to leave, but one of the employees walked through the store just to make sure everything was clean. He had a surprise waiting for him in the PlayPlace when he walked in. The child that ordered food, about five to six hours prior was still playing with no parent in sight. He was asked where his parent was, and the kid didn't know. The employee brought the kid into the dining room and, a little while later, his mother showed up. The employee unlocked the door for the parent to come inside, and he politely told her that she can't just leave her kid in the PlayPlace because if no one checked, he would have been stuck in there all night. She snapped back with the classic parent rebuttal, by saying, "Don't tell me how to raise my kids!!"

I'm sorry, I forgot that leaving a young child at a playground or PlayPlace unsupervised is Parenting 101. Our bad!

"Boy Or Girl"

One evening, I was taking orders in the drive thru. This guy pulled up to the speaker and ordered a whole lot of food, including a kid's meal. We had toys for boys and girls so I asked him, "Is that kid's meal for a boy or a girl?"

The other end went dead so I thought he drove around and never heard the question. The next sounds I heard were of him, frantically calling his wife asking her what kind of child they had.

I wonder if he was even in the delivery room when it was born.

"The Terrors"

A few parents came in and had their kids play in the PlayPlace for hours while they just sat around and talked. One woman came in around 3 in the afternoon and stayed until 10 at night, with her son and just let him play while she did some sort of paperwork. She wouldn't pay any attention to him and he was able to do anything he wanted. A few hours later, their friends came in, and the other lady had a girl about the same age so the kids played together for the rest of the night. Well, the key idea is "they wouldn't pay attention to their kids." Their kids ran around the entire store and do what kids do when no one watches them, whatever they wanted. One night, they had measuring tape, string, and took about fifty straws. They tied all of the straws together, went to the top of the PlayPlace, let the string down, and started swinging from it. Since this is a hazard, I stopped it. I threw out the straws, string, and broken measuring tape. The kids told their parents this, and the parents just told them to wait until I left then they can just get it from the garbage. After I heard this, I decided to change the garbage bag. As I was leaving with it, the parent decided to stop me and told me that the measuring tape was hers and she wanted it. I said that since her kid had a history of rowdiness in the store, she needed to watch her kid or leave.

After a lot of fights with other kids, running around the store and into other customers, leaving garbage behind, screaming and yelling throughout the store, and just general disruption, it had to be stopped one way or another. They didn't just earn the nickname "The Terrors" by everyone at the store because they were pleasant.

"Birthday Party Blues"

One of my first birthday parties was quite brutal. It was for twenty eight kids and twenty eight adults. The PlayPlace only fit about twenty people in total so it was a bit cramped. It was like those cans of mini-wieners, no room to move and extremely loud. All by myself, I had to make all their drinks, set up all their food, and constantly clean and get them whatever they needed, with a smile on my face. Well, by the end of the night and after they left, there was no more smile, just an extremely tired person with nothing to show for it. When we have birthday parties, the person doing the parties is considered a waiter or waitress, a server. Well, it is customary to tip people that provide these types of services for you. No one told them this because they never tipped me. While cleaning up the mess from the piñata, yes they had a freaking piñata that exploded with candy and paper that went everywhere, I found a goody bag that they accidently left which I considered to be my tip. I worked hard all for a few pieces of candy that was then eaten by the manager and another employee.

Jeez, thanks guys.

Another party that I had wasn't one of the toughest parties that I had to do but it was one of the most emotionally consuming. The parents of a birthday party on a Friday night, the busiest night of the week, constantly complained about everything. They actually went up to the manager on duty and told him, "He's so slow. I don't have anything yet and this is the worst service I have ever had."

I know this because I was standing right behind her the entire time she was talking to that manager.

There are two things to consider. 1) It was a mad house in the store so making drinks and food is tough because it's coming from every direction.

2) It was a huge party and I am by myself and am still treated as if I am purposely trying to ruin their good time.

My favorite part was when she came up to me after the party and told me that I was "great" and tried to give me props for a superb birthday party.

Thanks for being patronizing! I mean that's what it's all about, being given praise I know you don't mean.

It is easy to say that I wasn't tipped there either.

In fact, the only time I was tipped for a birthday party was because she was guilt tripped into it. I had a small birthday party that had the minimum amount of kids attend. It was a relatively easy birthday party because there wasn't much food, drinks, or clean-up. After she came up to pay, the manager came over and was talking to her. He realized that I wasn't tipped and asked her how the party played out. She said that it was enjoyable and her kids had fun. He then asked how her service was in front of me and she said, "It was good. Oh and here's something for you."

She handed me seven dollars. It's quite sad that you have to be guilt tripped into tipping at all and making people feel appreciated for their hard work. I never did another party afterwards.

For the record, I did many other parties in between that didn't make the cut.

"Change Can Be a Bad Thing"

A guy came in at around dinner time with his son. The father parked on the same side of the drive thru cars was driving. As he was passing the windows, one of which people were paying, he saw that people were sometimes dropping their coins. A penny here, a dime there and realized that all of that change could add up to less than a dollar. He thought about it and said to himself, "Let's go for it!" That is when he came up with a plan that was just brilliant. He looked at his kid, then looked at the change, and then put one and one together. On his way into the store, he had his son grab change in between the cars in a "Frogger" style, and had his kid dodge cars. I hope the less than a dollar was worth being a horrible father.

Cheap and thrifty are nice words when describing this genius; moron is even better.

CHAPTER 4

I Can't Believe I Shouldn't Have Done That

"I'm Using Your Own Money to Pay for This Order"

Employees or customers dropped change on the ground every once in the while. If we dropped it, we gave the customer the rest of their change from the drawer and picked up the rest later. If they dropped it, we told them not to worry because we just picked it up later. This guy came through late at night and ordered something small and parked his car as far away from the window as he could. He then came to the window, picked up as much change as he could and tried to pay for his order in our money.

I'm sure you thought the guy who told his kid to pick up change was frugal, and you were right, but this guy has his photo next to cheap in the dictionary.

"I'm Missing the Food I Never Ordered"

We had a missing food list for patrons that came in and either forgot their food, or we got their order wrong. Well, one guy realized we practiced that and decided to take advantage of the system. He came in every once in a while but before he did, he called the store and complained saying that we forgot his whole meal. For a little while, we didn't say anything about it, and we gave it to him. After a while, there was a pattern with him when he came and was always on the list. Most of the time, the food he was missing was after he sat down, in the store, and ate it. His name was not allowed to be on the list, nor his wife, which of whom, did the same thing.

What's more romantic than a nice dinner paid for by a lie?

"Creamed"

This guy came through all the time, ordered a coffee, and wanted like 30 creamers or so with it. We all just thought he was just disgusting until the day that he came in the afternoon and ordered a chicken sandwich with fifty creams. That's when we knew he was really disgusting! We told him that it wouldn't be a problem and we would put the cream on his sandwich, but he refused. We asked him why he wanted the cream and he said that he didn't care for our coffee and he used it for his own coffee at home. We told him that if he wanted creamers that he needed to purchase them, and we only gave him a reasonable amount for free.

He didn't care for the fact that he had go to the store to purchase cream.

"Action in the Bathroom"

One normal afternoon, or what was thought to be a normal afternoon, we received an interesting complaint. A customer came up to the counter, and she said that there was commotion in the ladies bathroom. Of course, there was no understanding of what kind of commotion and so a manager went to check up on the complaint. To their surprise, there was a lot of "fun" happening. They walked up to the bathroom door and knocked. After hearing the giggles, they realized there were two girls, both in a stall, and as adult Ralphie would say from *A Christmas Story*, they were "going at it like two jack rabbits on a hot date," or in other words having sex.

Imagine being told to leave the bathroom after being caught with your panties down.

"Late Night 'Snack'"

Late one night, these two girls came in and went straight to the bathroom. On their way to the bathroom, they were chatting really loudly. One girl said to the other, "I really need to have sex!"

I, being the man I was, was thinking just as loudly, "Right here! I got a break coming up!"

Remember, I said I was thinking it, but alas, they didn't hear my thoughts, came and left.

"Can I Have the Strip Club?"

Late one night, this guy came inside to order a sandwich. I told him what the total was, and really causally while looking out the window, asked me, "So, do you know where the closest "Strip Club" is?"

I responded, "And nineteen cents is your change…. Um, what was that?"

His buddy was outside waiting for the directions because he didn't want to come in and didn't want to look like a perv.

Now, I knew darn well where the closest strip club was, but being eighteen years old, you don't want to seem like you do know it off the top of your head; it's a matter of keeping face. So, my manager and I waited about a second before telling him that it was right down the street, on his right.

"Hit On and Run"

Late one night, I was on the close shift. It became time for either my closing partner or me to take orders in drive thru. We decided who was going to take orders in drive thru by flipping a coin and I lost. The first car that came through was a bunch of young, male adults. After I took the order, took their money and gave them their food, one of them in the backseat looked at me in the eye and said, "My friend just wanted to let you know that he thinks you're very cute."

I've never been hit on by another man before. In fact, I've never been hit on by another human before. I didn't know to respond, being straight and all, as well as not wanting to hurt their feelings, so I did what anyone in my spot would do. I said, "Thanks but I'm sorry, I'm not interested." And I closed the window.

"A Little Over Joyed"

This is a nice little story in the middle of mayhem. One night, this lady who didn't speak English came through the drive thru. The only person with any Spanish speaking ability at the time was me so I took her order. She was overjoyed with me after I took her order and because someone spoke her language that she started saying, "Te quiero. Mi amor. Gracias." When translated into English it means, "I love you. My love. Thank you." Everyone that heard it started laughing.

I don't know at what the laughter was for because she was pretty cute.

"Thank God That's My Cell Phone"

Once in a while, organizations in the community looked for sponsorship, and we helped those organizations. Sometimes, it was schools, churches, or other benefits. Well, one Sunday morning, a local church was doing a picnic that afternoon and wanted to know if we were interested in donating them some ice. We did it with no problem, and I knew the church because it was one that I attended for the longest time. I didn't know the guy getting the ice but I had seen him around. I was in the back, as he and his helper, were putting the ice into bins, and we were just talking. He was asking me questions like, "How long have you been working here?" and "Where do you live?"

I thought this was just casual conversation until I realized that his hand was sliding up the side of my leg. He grabbed the side of my pants and it was at that point that I excused myself. I needed to get away from the creep.

I don't know what he thought he grabbed, but I was glad it was just my cell phone.

"I Love You"

One afternoon, this young lady came through the drive thru. I walked over to hand her food she ordered, and she looked at me and said, "Damn there are some hot guys working in the drive thru!" I immediately started looking around thinking, "Where?"

I heard her but I asked her what she said anyway. She looked at me and said she didn't say anything. I was guessing she was kind of embarrassed at what she said so loudly. I didn't mind it, though; I like having my ego stroked. I then proceeded to give her the rest of her order and she turned to me and said, "I love you!" I guess she really did say something before.

Without thinking, I just looked at her and said, "Thank you! It's nice to hear things like that!" especially when you rarely ever hear that.

"J-E-L-L-O"

Now, I have heard this twice so it can't be just a coincidence.

A female employee walked to the bathroom during her shift and on her way back, an older guy, by older I mean could be her grandfather, called her over. He needed her to know that he loved the way "her butt jiggled when she walked." It must have been "mesmerizing?"

Another time, someone else's behind was compared to Jell-O.

This is completely unacceptable behavior from men said to women. As some men may think it's cute or funny, it would be surprising to those guys that women don't like it or think it's amusing, and if you don't believe me, ask them yourself. Remember, the quickest way to a woman's heart is through her stomach, not the weird comparisons that you can make about their body to some sort of food you would love to put in your mouth.

Just a quick thought while on the subject of catcalling. I was catcalled a few years ago. I was at the beach and this woman shouted to me, "Hey you, yeah you!"

I'm thinking, "Well this is weird but let's see what she wants.

She finished by saying, "Yeah, put a shirt on, no one wants to see that!"

Oh well, can't win them all!

"Wear Unbunching Underwear"

When I first started working there, I had a really early in the morning shift and these old guys came in to order. They walked up and placed their order. They gave me a hard time by messing with me and complaining about everything under the sun. They obviously knew they ticked me off, but as a young kid, what would you expect with unruly customers. On their way out, I was cleaning the doors and windows, and they came up to me and told me "not to get my panties in a bunch." I guess they saw themselves as the hero in this saga as they did their rude customer antics for me to make me see how people can act.

The rest of the day I was thinking, "What made them think that I was wearing panties?" I love how others can think everyone is a cross dresser! (Not that there's anything wrong with it)

CHAPTER 5

When You Ask a Stupid Question...

"I Would Like Some Dirt and Pine Needles with My Coffee"

Early one morning, this older gentleman drove in a parking spot. He walked throughout the parking lot and looked through all the garbage cans for something. He finally found what he was looking for, an old discarded coffee cup. He then brought the coffee cup inside and asked for his free refill. Now, we did refills on dine-in customers only. So, if you came through drive thru or left the store, you can no longer get a refill. We looked inside the cup, and there was still dirt and pine needles inside the cup. He didn't even wash out the cup! There are very few times that this rule is ever bent, but who wouldn't want to see this guy drink dirt. It was kind of like a "dare" he did to himself because he was cheap. He got his "refill" and drank it down.

Be careful what you ask for because you may drink dirt.

"But I Bought That a Few Days Ago"

Someone walked in through the door with a coffee cup and walked up and asked for a refill. Now, we do free refills after you pay for coffee. We told him that he had to pay for the drink and as he explained it, he bought it a few days and now wants his refill. We told him, again, that he needed to pay for the coffee in order to get the refills. So the customers that sat behind his general area decided to chime in and defend him that we should give him the refill because we do it for everyone else.

1) That's not true; we don't do it for everyone else.
2) If everyone that came in only had to bring a cup, why charge for drinks? It makes little to no sense. Here's to handouts that people think they deserve.

"Size Does Matter!"

This is keeping with the stories about refills; refills are for dine in customers only. A guy ordered some food in drive thru and a small diet coke. He downed the diet coke like he was dying of thirst, and then handed the cup back to us to refill it. We told him we didn't do refills through the drive thru and he became immediately indignant on us telling us we had to refill his soda. He asked what he was supposed to do and we said we could get him some water. Unfortunately, water was too healthy of a choice.

Next time you're thirsty to the point of downing your beverage, order a bigger size, if it's legal to do so of course.

"Age Does Matter?"

This guy walked in during lunch, and he placed his order. After the order was taken, he asked me my age. He then turned around and started asking all of the customers behind him in line how old they thought I was. My thoughts were like an altered version of The Ting Tings song, "That's Not My Name."

They kept saying, "I think your nineteen! I think you're twenty! I think you're thirty!"

I kept thinking, "That's not my age. That's not my age!"

It's weird to have a full room of adults trying to guess the age of someone just trying to serve them food.

"Get Out the Way, Get Out the Way"

One morning, this guy with a tractor trailer truck parked his car between the drive thru and parking spots. It was blocking the exit so no one could leave. After a little while, we realized that his truck wasn't waiting for traffic to subside but it was because he just wanted to be a jerk and not walk a few more feet. We noticed his inconvenience because we saw a few cars had to turn around and exited using the entrance. After he left, we received phone calls that told us about how a truck blocked the exit. He soon left after being a complete jerk.

If you're reading this, thanks man, keep it up!

"The Parked Truck HIT My Car"

Once upon a time, we received a delivery from our supplier. They sent trucks with our logo on it so they were quite distinguishable from any other tractor trailers. It parked on the entrance side of the drive thru with parking spots to the right of it and people drove around it to enter the drive thru line. The truck driver put the brakes on and got out to help us unload our items to make his stop faster. Well, one genius, written sarcastically, decided that today was the day that they wouldn't pay attention to what they were doing. When they backed out of their spot, they stayed in reverse and hit the truck. That's right! They backed up into the truck! They got out of their car, and walked up to the manager and truck driver, and yelled at the driver for hitting their car.

Now, you tell me. How does someone, who is outside of their truck and their truck is parked, get into an accident where it is their fault? Just another example of "it's always someone else's fault!"

"Living on the Edge" ("Hanging on a Moment of Truth")

The store next to us was an auto parts store. Separating us was a small grassy gnoll, but it was on elevated ground probably a foot or two high. One afternoon, there was traffic on the road which backed up the exit. One car in line to leave was a jeep with a risk taker in the driver's seat. He decided that it would be faster and easier to drive over the grass to the auto parts store and leave using their exit, not realizing that the ground was much lower on the auto parts side. I'm sure you guessed it. He got stuck, with a wheel of his jeep hanging over the auto parts store. They had nothing in their store to get his truck down. Shortly after doing something so dumb, the kids called for a tow truck. A police officer was also on route after being notified by someone there because of this stunt. The police arrived first and issued a few tickets. During this time, we learned that this specific driver already had many points on his license, and it was about to be taken away. He should have waited the five minutes to use our exit instead of the hour and a half it took for the tow truck to get it down.

Upside- No one got hurt, and it was a great photo op day for many who had never seen that before, including myself.

"Power Lines"

I know this may not be a customer story but what the hay. We had a pharmacy/convenience store across the street. Well, one morning, their delivery truck left on a downhill part of the road, and right above the street were power lines. So, the power lines were too low, the truck was too high, or luck was just bad, but the roof of the truck hit the power lines and ripped them out of the ground. I mean, it ripped all of the wooden stakes out of the ground like it was nothing. It took out power for us as well as everything around us.

You don't realize how much technology and electricity means to businesses and society until you no longer have it. Never have I seen so many sparks; it felt as if I was in a Michael Bay movie, no real plot, just explosions.

CHAPTER 6

Then You Look Stupid

"In America, Everything Gets Cheese"

This was actually a relative of mine many years ago when he worked in fast food. Someone walked up to the counter and began to order a vanilla shake and, all serious, asked if they could have some cheese in the shake. They looked at him like, "Really, dude? That's **REALLY** what you want?"

Well, of all the disgusting things people could think of experimenting with, that person won!

This ranks just underneath chocolate cover ants.

"Not Everything Is About You"

This guy walked up to the counter trying to improperly use a coupon. When he was told how to use it, he liked his way better but used it. He was upset but seemed to let it go, well, at least for a little while. Well, he eventually sat down, and enjoyed his meal. The employee that took his order started talking to another employee about their schedule, and this guy believed they were talking about him so he got up and yelled at them for talking about him. When he left, they were stunned and confused because no one ever said anything about him.

Remember, not everything people talk about is about you! Once in a while they talk about other people, instead!

"Get a Real Job"

One late night, these two customers came through the drive thru and tried to place their order. I asked them what they would like to have. Their response was, "Hold on a sec. I don't know what kind of sh*t they have. (Talking to the passenger) What the f*ck do you want to eat?"

The passenger replied, "I don't know. They have so much f*cking sh*t to choose from."

Now, I'm not going to say that I have never cursed or don't know what they were saying but when it comes to respecting others, especially at their job, just do it. Just give them respect whether you agree with it or not. After a few minutes of them going back and forth cursing like that, I told them to leave because I didn't feel comfortable taking their order. They demanded to talk to the manager and he heard the whole conversation and told them the same thing. They drove around and passed the window, but they didn't leave without screaming, "Get a real job!"

I didn't understand why they said that to me because I helped pay for the unemployment checks they probably received all the time.

"Good Old Fashioned Spanish Curse Off"

My friend worked the window one night when someone came through and ordered four or five meals. They separated the sandwiches and the fries because it could not fit in one bag. After my friend took the money and gave the drinks and sandwiches, he said to the guy, "Hold on a moment so I can get your fries."

Of course, he didn't pay attention, or understand, to what my friend said so he just drove away. He came back inside ten minutes later and started yelling at us in Spanish. Now, the managers spoke Spanish, and even they couldn't understand him. I said to the one manager, "What did he say?"

The manager replied to me, "I have no idea."

The only part of the conversation they understood was, "Mi casa es tu casa!" (Then pointing at someone else) "You too! You too!"

What he was trying to say, and this is the afterthought, is that when he got home, he was missing his fries that we told him to wait for, and he was saying "You too" to everyone so he wouldn't have to blame himself.

After that, he got the rest of his food and went home, but not before he cursed everyone off first. It was good for me because, at the time, I didn't know much Spanish.

See, paying attention to what you're doing pays off, or would pay off in this instance.

"Spring Ahead"

In NJ, like most of the US, during the spring, we have "Daylights Saving Time." In the spring, we jumped ahead an hour and there were always customers that didn't know how to do that. So we got customers at 11 a.m. that thought it was still 10 a.m. Well, this one guy came in, after we sprang ahead, and was belligerent about the current time. He said he wanted something off the breakfast menu and I told him that it was lunch, and we didn't serve that right now. He told me that it was well before 11 a.m. and how I have to do what he said. Eventually, he came up to the window, yelled at me, told me what I could go do with myself, and where to shove it. He left, never knowing the real time or how to respectfully treat others and it caught up with him.

About a week later, he had a heart attack with all the "stresses" of his life.

Long story short, if your life feels stressful, take a step back, take a deep breath, and don't curse everyone else off. It will make others less responsive in helping you with your problems if they feel pushed away.

And for the record, this sort of thing happened all the time in the fall after we "fell back" as well but with the exact opposite question, "Do you have lunch?"

"Don't Go In There"

Late one night, it was a bit slow. An employee needed to use the restroom and so they walked in the bathroom, did their business, and came back. After he came back, a customer walked in the store and went in the direction of the bathrooms, immediately ran out, and came up to the counter saying things like, "Oh my God! What died in there?!" and, "Whoever just used the bathroom needs to go see a doctor, NOW!"

He just sat back, listened to the complaints, and started laughing.

"Don't Drink and Drive… Or Drink and Order"

Late at night, this guy came through the drive thru, and it was clear that he had a few too many drinks. You could smell it on him. Clearly, drinking and driving could get someone killed, anyone killed, so we did the only noble thing that anyone should do; we told him his fries were going to take a few minutes to cook, told him to pull up, and we would bring it out to him when they're done. Of course, during that time we weren't cooking fries, but the police came out and took him away for being well over the legal limit.

"Family Member Mayhem"

We had an employee with a crazy family. He had an especially nutty aunt that drove everyone up the wall. Many people's first encounter with the "Queen of Crazy" was when she came in to order. No one, not an employee, a manager, or anyone else, could make her happy, even after many attempts at trying. Everyone's aim was to not make her mad. For example, she came up and ordered nuggets. Now, you're thinking, "Simple enough? Right?"

Well, she demanded that they be fresh which is understandable, the fresh part, not the demanding part. So we started making new ones and after the three and a half minutes of cooking, they were ready. She stared the entire time at the people that were making them to ensure that they had gloves on and they used tongs. She took the food that she ordered and sat down with it. Immediately, after she tasted the product, she came up with the food and told us that it was not fresh and that she wanted new food. We reassured her that it was fresh, especially after she watched it cook. So for the first few times, we humored her. It was made again, and she got it again. If it didn't meet her approval again, she came back up. She screamed and yelled at whomever she could find. Her new complaint was that since she had to wait for newer nuggets, her fries were now cold. It would always a "lose-lose" situation that even her nephew hated when she showed up. This happened with her to the point that every time she walked up to the door, you could hear someone scream the phrase, "Run! She's coming!" and everyone would run and hide.

I have personally seen this person also harass banks, other restaurants, and supermarkets. Please, don't be this person!

The other thing she would do was...

There were times when she called the store because she wanted to talk to him. He reluctantly accepted, taking one for the team, most of the time. Sometimes, he told the manager that he wasn't there if she called. Things got interesting because she would not hang up until she spoke with him. Those times we just hung up on her, and she called right back and asked, "Did you just hang up on me?"

We responded, "I don't know. Did it sound something like this?" Click.

On days that he wasn't there, she still called looking for him. If you told her that he wasn't there, she called you a liar then showed up at the store. Although when she entered the store, you always heard the phrase, "Run! She's coming!"

Please, don't be this person!

HONORABLE MENTIONS!

The "Honorable Mentions" category happens so frequently that these stories deserve their own section! I also like to call this the rapid fire of stupidity!

Customer: Can I have a hamburger?
I don't know... Can you?

Customer: Does your cheeseburger have cheese on it?
I don't know. Let me go check...

(After ordering just a sandwich)
Customer: Did you put ketchup in the bag?
Did you ask for ketchup in the bag?

Customer: Could I order a chicken sandwich?
Crew: Is that grilled or crispy chicken?
Customer: Yes.
I didn't realize that was a yes or no question.

Crew: Ok, so would you like anything else today?
Customer: Yes. (Waits a few seconds) I'm done.
It seems like you answered that correctly.

(In the drive thru)
Crew: Ok. Is there anything else I can get you?
Customer: No thank you, but that will be to go!
You're in the drive thru, right? So how is that not "for here?"

Customer: Can I get a barbeque sauce?

Crew: Sure. (Hands him a sauce)

Customer: Oh and a mustard. (Gets sauce) Oh and ketchup. (Gets sauce) And honey mustard....

If you need multiple things, it is legal to ask for them all at once.

(Drives past the speaker and up to the window)

Customer: Sorry, didn't even see the speaker there.

If you miss obvious things like that then I don't want to be on the same road as you... I'm sure you're the one asking the cop after he pulls you over, "When did they put the red light there?"

And the cop will be all like, "20 years ago!"

Customer: (Comes up with a sandwich wrapped in a "hamburger" wrap in hand) I said I wanted a cheeseburger without cheese on it not a hamburger!

Even vegetarians and vegans can laugh at this one. Also, that happens to every new crew person. Somehow, no one ever can understand the subtle differences.

Customer: (directed towards the person in the window) Any chance I could get your number?

Crew: Sorry, I don't date customers. Against company policy!

That's one way to get them off your back! And if it were true, we would all be single!

Customer: Man, I'm so high...

Crew: That's how we manage to stay in business.

Thanks for walking here too.... Worst case scenario is that you get pulled over for walking while under the influence....

(In drive thru)

Crew: Alright, would you like anything else?

Customer: Nah, that's it for now.

Are you coming back for dessert or something? Because I can get it for you now to save you a trip back...

Customer: Alright, here is my money…. (Crew takes it and immediately after opening the register) Why was my total it so much?

Really? You chose now to ask that question. Not say, before you paid?

(Customer brings up their chicken sandwich after taking a bite out of it)

Customer: Is it too late to ask for this without the lettuce?

You took a bite out of it… What do you think?

Crew: Hi! What can I get for you today?

Customer: Yeah, I want a hahaha. And a hehehe.

Please don't let your kids order. It's a business, not a daycare! It's not cute, it's annoying!

Customer: (Walks in with bag in hand) This isn't my order!

Crew: I'm sorry! What was wrong with it that I can fix?

Customer: That's not the point! Every time I come here it's always wrong and no one can ever get anything right!

So, three things: 1) You should never say this "happens every time" ever to anyone because you have to ask yourself, "Why do I keep coming here?" especially when you claim incompetence. It shows your competence. 2) Communication is a two way street. Maybe there was a communication error which both parties share blame. 3) You always get a lot further being nice to others than being a jerk. (Trust me)

Crew: (Handing two bags of food to the customer) Alright, I have your drinks coming in a second.

Customer: Where are my drinks?

I'm sorry. What did I just say? We were only born with two hands.

Crew: Hold on a second for you drinks.

Customer: (Zoom! And they're out of here)

Customer: (They return after a few minutes to get their drinks) I was just here and you never gave me my drinks.

No, you were just here and booked it out of here without the drinks! Paying attention always pays off in the long run.

Customer: (Places order really fast)
Crew: I'm sorry, what did you want again?
Customer: (Places order really slowly thinking you're stupid)
I've always kind of wondered if people understand that it's the same price regardless how long it takes to place the order. Sometimes, I think that there are some people hoping to start a new game for the Olympics and call it the "Ordering Quickly at Fast Food Because We Have Nothing Better To Do" team.

Customer: The coffee I just ordered is too hot…
Different Customer: The coffee I just ordered is too cold…
Sometimes I feel like Goldilocks when dealing with people and their coffee. It is NEVER just right!

(Customer walks in)
Customer: I was here yesterday and never got my food.
Crew: Did you call?
Customer: I didn't know I had to call.
Crew: Do you have a receipt or anything that says you were here yesterday?
Customer: No but you forgot it.
I didn't realize we all could just walk into any store, claim you never received your goods, and just expect to get it for free. This is going to make my Holiday shopping much easier and cheaper!

(As we opened in the morning)
Customer: Is your coffee fresh?
I don't know; we did just open.

(Customer ordered food with a large Coke and large Orange Hi-C. After handing him the Coke)
Customer: Is this the Orange Hi-C?
Yes, because the **ORANGE HI-C** is now brown. As Bill Engvall would say to this guy, "Here's your sign!"
And if you don't know who that is, shame on you. Look him up!

MY HOPE

My hope from writing this is to get people to understand. I hope people will understand that their actions every day and every moment affect other people. From the time you wake up to the time you go to sleep, everything you do has a repercussion on this planet. Every action. Every word. Every smile. Every frown. Every dirty look. Every hug. Every kiss. Every time you wake up is another day to make a difference in someone's life. It can be for the good. It can be for the bad. It is what you make it; every action and every word that comes from you will determine what kind of day it will be, for you, your family and friends, and for all of the people around you, as well as all of those to come. You should strive to leave this world a little bit better off than when you came into it, and guys, with the toilet seat down.

Remember, you're not alone in this world; there are a few other people around you. We must all work together in order to take this world from being war torn to a utopia. We must realize we are not all enemies working for ourselves, but friends working to better each other in a way that will benefit all of us. When you help others, in the long run you help yourself. Live. Love. Cherish each moment. Hope for a brighter tomorrow. These are all aspects of life we should all strive to emulate, while, once again guys, keeping the toilet seat down.

FINAL THOUGHTS

In my humble opinion, the hardest job on the planet is anything that deals with the general public. Whether you work in a restaurant as any kind of server, or hold a public servant job, it is very difficult to deal with many different personalities on a daily basis. Dealing with hundreds to thousands of personalities a day is difficult because people like to be treated differently. There is one common thread between every single person that deals with the general public and that is the ability to adapt. Adapting to different people, different cultures, and different languages on a daily basis is the key to thriving in that atmosphere.

So, this is a piece of advice to anyone who reads this; be kind to anyone in these types of jobs or careers. They already deal with a lot (they are normal people with private lives) and don't need more baggage from you, and realize that something so small, like a smile will go a long way to making their day go from horrible to great, or creepy, in a matter of seconds.

A good second piece of advice: Be kind to everyone! You don't know who might just be interviewing you for a job you want in the future and probably don't want to be labelled as the person who cursed them off or gave them a hard time. We all want to be accepted and appreciated and being kind will demonstrate what we strive for: acceptiated! (accepted + appreciated)

EXTRAS

"Fifty Shades of Priesthood"

One of our regulars came in on what I thought to be a normal morning. He ordered his usual, sat down, and ate it. On his way out, he walked up to me and handed me fifty dollars and said that I was always very pleasant. He told me that I should think about becoming a priest and that his parish was looking for more young people to be spreading the Word of God. I thought to myself, "I sin every day, especially, in that impure thoughts category. How could I become a priest? More importantly, I didn't want to become a priest!"

I told him I would think about it because that's the nicest possible way to get out of the conversation, but every time he came in he would ask me about it. Eventually, I had to dodge him in order to dodge the conversation.

"Sex Solves Everything"/ "Don't Shoot 'Em Up"

In the morning, this guy, came through the drive thru and made inappropriate remarks to me. One morning, I was tired, and we were busy. He saw that I was tired and thought I was in a bad mood so he told me I should ask to go home so I could have sex and then would be refreshed and the problem, solved.

When was the last time someone did that at work? Asked their boss if they could go home to have sex then return? As a manager, I couldn't explain the weirdness I would have after hearing someone say to me, "I'm not feeling happy. Can I go home and get laid? I'll be back in half hour!"

A few weeks later, that same guy returned for a second dose of ridiculous words coming out of his mouth. He ordered his iced coffee with very exact amounts of milk and if it was off by even the slightest, you had to start over again. It was made twice and neither was to his satisfactory. I got agitated so I told him that I would put everything on the side and he could make it. After I told him that he replied, "Whatever you want to do, just don't come back and shoot the place up!"

That type of person can easily agitate me but as soon as he left, I turned into the nice guy that I know I am.

"Lawsuits"

This made headlines at one point, if you consider page 3 as part of the headlines. This guy walked in on a weekday afternoon during the school year. He ordered some food, ate the food while reading the newspaper, left his table a complete mess, and then left. The manager saw this all transpire, and decided to politely ask him to clean up his mess. He walked out of the store as the manager walked up to him. He became furious that someone dared ask him to clean up his mess and felt that we were getting paid to clean up after him. He became so unruly that, as a precaution with children in the building, he decided to lock the doors so that he couldn't come in and nothing more would happen. The guy started banging the doors attempting to gain entrance. Soon afterwards, he got in his car and left. On his way to wherever he was going, he got into an accident and hit a pole.

He told the police that he had an incident with the manager after he ate and that was distracting him as he drove. It became the manager's fault that this guy's actions and quick to anger resulted in a taken down pole. Eventually, the owner found out he was being sued for this whole incident.

A few years later, when the story hit the courts and the local newspapers, we got to learn his side of the story. He told everyone how scarred he became because of the whole incident, and he even had nightmares every time he sees the golden arches. He sued for millions of dollars and received something for his troubles. His lawyer fees were the only thing that got paid.

Yes, one person asking someone else not to be a pig is called an "incident."

"I Need Some Air"

The gas station next to us had an air pump that pumped out free air for tires. Well, the gas station closed down, and there was yellow "Do Not Enter" tape around the entrances. This guy must have really needed air for his tires. Between us and the gas station there is a grassy incline and a sidewalk. This genius thought, "Well, if I can't get in the gas station, let me back up on to the hill and get in from the side."

He thought that then did that. He backed his car up on the grass to get to the pump. I saw this and walked outside and told him to get off of the grass. He looked at me and said in whatever accent he had, "Just give me a minute!"

I told him to move now because he was crushing the grass. Some people have no shame, honestly!

The worst part is that there was a gas station across the street that he could have filled his car's tire with air for 75 cents-ish. Although, doing that was too expensive.

"You Made It Myself"

These two old ladies walked in for iced coffees. They wanted a very specific amount of milk and Splenda in it that the person taking the order tried to make it. It was too light and sweet after just putting a small amount in it. He made it a second time but put nothing in it and got them packets of cream and Splenda and told them that if they needed more they could come up and he would give them more. Well, they came up a few minutes later with their iced coffees and told him that he made them too sweet and creamy. He told them that he put nothing inside the coffee and they insisted for another.

If you're going to blame someone because you did something wrong, make it more convincing than they did.

"Diet Water"

This woman came through and she asked for diet water. Now, the order taker was taken back a bit by this because she had never heard of anything like that. To be fair, I don't think there are many people that would've been able to say, "Yes, I've heard of that!"

She said that they didn't have any diet water and the woman didn't understand why. She inquired as to why we didn't carry it and told us that the local grocery store carried it. She said she would return with a diet water to prove it was real.

First off, I don't know what "diet water" could possibly be. I thought water was as diet of a drink you could possibly get. Secondly, we're not a grocery store and don't carry everything they carry in a store.

"Yell At Me"

This guy came through the drive thru and started asking for things we don't have on the menu. He was asking for things our competitors sold that we didn't sell. He eventually went with the 2 for $3. She accidently put 2 orders in which was wrong and you know what that means, castration. He eventually told her that he didn't want 2 orders of it and she told him she would fix it and to just drive around. She fixed it and he drove around and didn't say a word to her. She took the money then he pulled up to the next window to pick up his food and the young lady tried to be nice to him and said to him in a calm, clear voice, "Hi! How are you today?"

In a scared, bewildered voice he told her, "Stop yelling at me!"

She responded, "I'm not yelling at you!"

He quipped, "I like being yelled at!"

Whatever floats your boat, chief!

"Doggy Dearest"

This one beautiful afternoon, we had a few women in line when another woman walked in the store and right up to the counter. She wanted to speak to the manager, and I said I was the manager on duty. She told me that there was a car parked outside with a dog in the car and a window barely cracked. She wanted to know who owned the car. Well, the owner of the car was in line and overheard what we were talking about and decided to speak up a little bit. The woman told the owner that if she didn't take care of her dog that she would call the police and the cops would come up with a solution to the situation because it was animal cruelty. The owner of the vehicle told her she only came in for something really quick and to leave her alone. Another customer took the owners side and said that it was a cool day out and the dog would be fine in there. The woman refused to leave until the owner of the dog left with him and lied in wait to call the police on her.

I may not be a dog owner but even I wouldn't do this to a beloved pet. Since most cars have windows on the car it becomes very hot because the windows "greenhouse" the heat. It may be a beautiful day out but that doesn't mean anything. The gentle breeze doesn't go through windows, no matter how transparent they are.

A video went viral that a doctor showed how quickly a car can become very hot and how uncomfortable anyone or anything would be living in that environment. So, if you do decide to go to the drive thru with the pet you love, actually use the drive thru, or leave them home.

"Stupid Punk Kids, Nowadays"

These two guys walked in on a Saturday morning and started placing an order with the crew person that was up front. The one guy wanted an iced coffee and told the person taking the order to put it in the normal large soda cup because they were much bigger. I happened to be walking up front and the crew asked me if he was allowed to do that for them. I told him that the iced coffee cups were different, and he had to use the iced coffee cup. When the guy heard that he became all sorts of pissed off. He told me, "Not giving him exactly what he wanted was the worst customer service you could have." He continued with the classic oldie but goodie, "Everyone does this all the time."

I told him, "Listen, that's not how it works. We have cups that specifically fill these drinks and people don't normally do what he asked us to do."

They tried to be snippy with me and talked down to me. After a few minutes of them telling me how ignorant that I am, they told me that "the customer is always right" so that means they were right. I told them that apparently that wasn't the case, and he looked as if he orgasmed in his mouth a little bit because he wanted something to complain about to attempt to get me fired. They asked for my name and I gave them my first name. They demanded a refund and I gave it to them. During the time it took me to refund their order, they decided to call me names, like a "punk kid" and attempted to run down my character to tempt me to get one last burst of cruelness out of me. I said nothing except, "Thanks for coming by!" to them because when you are nice to someone when they are being nasty to you purposely, they tend to become more irate that they couldn't anger you and makes them more angry when they see you are happy.

They didn't get the full reaction that they desired but did call later to take their frustrations out on another manager. They told the next manager that they came in and were angels and that I was the big, bad punk kid that was being rude for no reason.

It is amazing how the story changes and does a complete 360 degrees when being explained by completely rude people. They didn't want to let the manager know what they did so I became the villain of the story.

Shout out to those guys! No one treats others like crap quite like you do, my friends!

"Later That Night"

This guy came in one night and placed a decently sized order to go. He had a big box of nuggets along with a couple meals. We got his food and drinks ready then he looked through his order, and after, left with his food. About **FOUR** hours later, he came back inside and walked up to the register where the manager was and told him that he never got his big box of nuggets. He had his receipt with him proving that he paid for it and then he pointed to me and told me I "messed up" his order that he placed **FOUR** hours earlier, inside the store. I told the manager I didn't remember the order at first so he gave him a refund for the nuggets. A few minutes after he left, I remembered the order and told the manager that I put everything in two bags and handed it to him. Half of his order was in one bag and the other half was in a second bag. If he was missing his nuggets, he was missing other things as well. Either he placed his order wrong, or, more likely, he wanted free food.

When you walk inside and are not driving, you can set your food at a table to check that you have everything. He checked his bags and saw everything in them and decided to leave. It shouldn't take **FOUR** hours for you to realize you're missing food. Also, walking through the door and making accusations against people doesn't make you seem all the more innocent. Just because you point your finger at someone else, doesn't mean you're right; it just means you're good at pointing.